# DAYS OF UNWILLING

## CAL BEDIENT

saturnalia books

# DAYS OF UNWILLING

## CAL BEDIENT

saturnalia books

Other books by Cal Bedient

**Poetry**

*The Violence of Morning*
*Candy Necklace*

**Literary Criticism**

*The Yeats Brothers and Modernism's Love of Motion*
*In the Heart's Last Kingdom: Robert Penn Warren's Major Poetry*
*He Do the Police in Different Voices*
*Eight Contemporary Poets*
*Architects of the Self: George Eliot, D.H. Lawrence, and E.M. Forster*

Saturnalia Books
13 E. Highland Ave., 2 Floor
Philadelphia, PA 19118
info@saturnaliabooks.com

ISBN: 0-9754990-9-2
Library of Congress Control Number: 2008925542

Book Design by Saturnalia Books
Printing by Westcan Printing Group, Canada

Cover Art: The Martyrdom of St. Matthew by Caravaggio (San Luigi dei Francesi, Rome)

Distributed by:
University Press of New England
1 Court Street
Lebanon, NH 03766
800-421-1561

The author wishes to thank the editors of the following journals in which many of these poems first appeared, often in different form: *American Letters & Commentary, Boston Review, Colorado Review, Conduit, CutBank, 88, Harvard Review, Hunger Mountain Review, LIT, New American Writing, 1913: A Journal of Forms, Pool, Seneca Review, Southern Review, VOLT*. "Polyester Perversities" appeared on the *Perihelion* web site.

Special thanks to Forrest Gander, Jorie Graham, Brenda Hillman, Susan McCabe, and 'Annah Sobelman.

# CONTENTS

—a detour, a dogged detour, in itself transitory and precarious, and deprived of any significance. Why, in that of its manifestations called man, does something happen, which insists throughout this life, which is called meaning? We call it human, but are we so sure? . . . when we get to the root of this life, behind the drama of the passage into existence, we find nothing besides life conjoined to death.

—Jacques Lacan

## WHAT THOUGH YOUR DADDY'S TRUMPET IS BUTTERED TOAST?

Very quietly he spoke: "You ain't fit to have him."
She looked up from the loom. It's about her milk.
Her robe plastered, transparent, to her breasts.

Not Odysseus, his arm pits orange as the slick
threads matting a pumpkin's seeds.
The sea itself spreads white flowers,
awaiting him. Him! His shoreward eyes:
handkerchiefs sopped with tears.

Murder isn't a compositor's cliché
to men whom Poseidon has schooled
in the wave theory of everything. See

how they row the last hexameter
in vowels anxious and looking back.

What use are shores, o mariner?

"I am waving the clear water of my hands."

# ALISON THANK YOU FOR YOUR QUESTION

Figures undifferentiated from their ground,
like hair curlers and a paper-towel-
floweret-patterned nightgown in the pubic kitchen

dusk? Like the languishing theory
of pogroms, seeing that "an object of history
cannot be targeted at all

within the continuous elapse of history"?
Was that the question, dear?

Yes, even if it's female of the landscape
to sway into forms, like a well
trained soprano's scream, a scream

is still a scream. The ground of things
shivers under the jerked-out texts

of the guns, of which
the shivering is the message, don't you agree?

I base my thinking on Benjamin's
Arcades Project and how glass

architecture is a late stage of development,
scholastic and deceptively open,

compared to which
a woman's love is "luxuriant sap," which is why

the branches twist, compared to which
"barbarism lurks in the very concept of culture."

Made by burning, the building is burning.

## CHORUS HERALDING ITSELF OUT OF THE IMPERIAL REDUNDANCY
## OF RAIN AGAINST THE SOBBING BREATH OF THE TIDE

would it be selfish to be prominent like geometry, or Melville
riding giddap on Hawthorne's shoulders? don't you wish to god
you could sing out? When I listen to poets reading their work
it's like hearing one of Titian's faces speak,
the meat wiped up, the muse's head carried under the arm
light as a paper moon. If we, too, babied the lamp
would it still be here, the syphilis, would it still be here, the offensive,
the floods of unspooling blood, would we smile, then,
another wife, would we open the door of the ambulance and see
there the road, there the mulberry trees, there two girls
why are they sniffling it happens when you love down
so bad, so bad. If *Dolce* goes off again to a little place
quadrilaterally sullen, with two suitcases, both of them crying,
will we have the stuff to stay behind?
We are tired of those will help each other
not much either. You listen to me, Undine:
the world isn't water, nor all the years between.

# ROSES COME AT ME BARKING LIKE LITTLE DOGS

I love all things straining at their leash of blood:
poets, for instance, the barflies and crop-

haired barbies of the Rose.
But not the eye, unable to tell

is that a painted canyon under a rough girl
or a rough canyon under a painted girl.

(Not girls thought it was girls,

don't resemble address,
splashes anything.)

Nor the ear, that yellow tube
waiting out front everyday
for *The Missoulian*

(can you hear the blind deer
biting thunder, like
an artichoke arrogantly aroused?)

Mouth, o mouth, we have to talk:
*my word! I couldn't  my breath  you taught me private . . .*

Like the shadow of a king in the room,
you amused yourself with me shamelessly.

       And you, heart, road to let:
let's lick the faces on stamps,
it will be so cat and irresponsible
toward evening's ruby telephone.
(God I'm not so good as.
Can't possibly be well.

How do I look?)

And *I, I, I,* the death vowel,
come to me single thing,

not so much fugitive, okay?
Snowing green alder leaves

on the river, and shipping,
shipping inhabitants.

(Take a peek, they told me,
handing me the key to the drawer.

We'll watch. Go on, they said, have a   )

And you with the blow-up sex doll
flying from your flag pole,

*do you miss your home tonight, soldier boy?*
Don't listen to Rose. Practice your
                              maneuvers.

Every nation's a murderer.
But enough about me.

# NOTICE TO THE PLAYERS

Most of you people rely too much on adscititious
aids to illusion.  The genius of surprise is alone the
Elenora Duse of it.  No doubt, the abraded silk
of Bernhardt's phthisical Camille
kerchiefing her lips in constant question
floats in the empyrean of the
pregnant handkerchief idea.  But Duse
hissed at the audience.  Was Juno
who never read a book in her life.

Be, don't read, the thing you'd play,
be grief, a hare inaudibly screaming.  Taste
in the syllables the murderous cakes your mother
baked in a kitchen where great green beans
stretched their legs from the painted chairs.
Walk onto the stage like wrath.  You are not
base born.  Who knows from how far you've come
into lights and color.
It's not who you are but what you are
I love, your shadows bowing wildly over the boards.

# YOU SMELL OF DIVES WHERE A PRICK LIKE YOU IS HATED

Once I peeked through your mail slot and caught a glimpse
of your quiet individual self-formed taste, the thousand pegs and pins.

I must have wanted you dead to see you like that.

You should always speak the little fires are in you.
I am not diseased with the remark. Love cares to see the blackened tongues.

You twitch with a gathering head stir. Yes, free the little speeds are in you.
You're a real person when you go crazy like that.

Their felt legs rolled up for carrying, your people stare from your pockets.
Stump round and round the world with them, they are your darlings,

they are not sparrows, they are not sparrows running like rats on the
    cloud sleeves.
Open your works-in-progress to them: let them choose their mausoleum.

The horses I could eat, if I still hungered for you.
Backcountry beauties farting lush grass.

# THE / 680 YEW GRAINS IN THE VOICE

a sterile easter
in the grass of THE.

in the grass of the THE
injugables tore the flies
not i tore the flies
to hear the little black
fountains of their voices.

the fountains made in pain
are torn as by one who tears an ass hole
to get to the mutt meat
of matter's mattering.

outside the THE
is horror,
       the clear core
        of the glass,
the tears coldy.

the nearest enterprise of THE
is the boulangerie
where the baker in DAWN apron
in the mutt dark
bakes the dry fountain of the Crumb.

the car that sailed into the river —
well, there are layers, layers
and different
breathings, thickest lowest down.

from the waters the lungs
blew like a child the balloon of
the balloon of

oh the breathtaking volupt
of the THE.

all together now they spread the day
like a sheet to catch
the Herculean solvents, the scalps
of intelligence, they set out the light
like buckets
        to harvest
the blood of the THE,
the THE without a "the."

if you could just feel it coming
and not
see a smoking maul,
        or something pale, unused, afraid.

# LOW WATER LETTER

It tears me from life to doubt
the absoluteness of this light
   wobbling in a basin,

               which trembles for you,
               gross Liebchen,
while white garden spiders flee from your feet—

such a *Relativitätsproblem* of a girl,
               your mood *noir* as Joan Mitchell's
turtle neck sweater as she paints
             *Chord VII* without any notes at all.

But who really sounds together anymore
at the precise times the composer indicates?

What I unconsciously write may fly around for a while
like a wolf *dans l'arbre de Mitchell*
when it thinks no one is looking,

but what I recognize in the choir
is the torn other cheek of the scale.

The transparent curtain almost raw fish in feel.

Absolute as a horse in grief.

## "YOU CAN BE THE SUBJECT OF WILD ADMIRATION IN TEN DAYS"

You could be terribly well put together.
The land has an eye to you. You're the very spirit of geography.
Don't fidget. Don't go striding above me, air spider.
Sit and talk away the evening. It's so hot.

You're the very spirit of occasions do skateboard about me.
Brilliant. Intensely desirable. Are you listening?
Your lipstick like watermelon split open on the rocks.
Don't fidget. Say what you feel. You'll like it.

Sustained notes, however, are out: their age, size, hunting dogs,
And code locations all dropped down
Like the hanged, whose many friends
Run to tug on their legs, they're that kind. Go

With feathers in the mouth, like the cat. It's called
Making it funky. (No, no, it is not for the lute to repeat.)
As I was saying, you're the understated darling of distances.
Eve. Evening. Evocative. Sit here with the bucket in your lap,

Hork if you must, but hush your sobbing—
Your chair throbs like a vibrator.
If my breath stinks of a hired gun, love me for it,
I could clear the prairie of hostiles.

What, you wander off? After all I've said?
I've met up with your kind before. I attract it, even.
Anyway, earth colors don't look good on you,

Do you know? And death, that fetishist, brings a dew

Slipper the size of your treacherous foot.

And after I had you where you smelled so good.

# THE PINK LETTER

When I understood that to touch somebody was to begin to die,

*I want your pink wine I want to meet you a stranger in the woods,*

it was too late. I had started with pink of child on a purple bike, I stood on the pedals on the down-stroke like angry brush work, then advanced caressing figure after figure, charming them out of the picture, washing them down Medicine River.

Now, when out of pink with local things, like a pause in conversation when the last words suddenly hear themselves jutting out from thought

*with a deep disquiet, because they knew Medusa had been listening,*

I long to be a pink flamingo but somewhere far from the horrid, water-shitting, stalky flock, with only the silk panties of the pink dawn around me. I know I could be happy if I weren't such a prick, a beggar who stands in front of the Rheims cathedral (I think that's me) and asks for something—anything—from the three gothic doors stiffed straight up like punk hair.

I could have been the grand multiplex sound of a waterfall, even, if I had kept my appointments with the strangers in the woods, in Canada,

*the caribou all the time rushing over your head like a thin wash of thunder sienna.*

But I drank the metaphor of beauty as a constant and considered goodness, I am radioactive with isotopes, *why am I being tested?*

*(a nude darting between trees years earlier).*

As for JJ,

> I disliked the way people raced by her
> as if she were nothing, like water in a pot
>
> hole, water-all-things come slapdash
> to the road.
>
> Hadn't I known her when she left for a year
> to live in a telescope with June?
>
> She was sensitive about it. My pupil
> was terrifying, probably. And the light
>
> practically ate too much of her.

A sea gull looking into the mirror remarked: "like a wedding, and a still life with horses."

There was not an acquaintance in the description who could name all the faces in it.

so many   so many   so many   so many:
you would not think there could be none. There are none. There are many.

Between in the mouth of among, exactly.
For Nature's a large quantity. Jane is Nature.
Therefore, Jane's a large quantity when the wee babies are in her and I
    paint her with young leaves, artificially.

Once I married a French gardener, on stilts, in a lemon skirt. Then I became a character in a novel. Then I was dead and alive again, inaugurating a carnal aura while sitting between Eva my right leg and Jessica my left.

My cat rubs his mouth against the piano leg and purrs like the wind
    when it excites itself with a hundred poplars.

The wind Jane, when all her whiskers are between.

The evident affectation of the foregoing passage, its indulgent fondness for non-identity, its thesis that there are no subjects, only processes, underlines the fact that modern art has lost its courage for the unitary, as when a paper bird flies into the shredder in full-throated *oh this harm of being one*. Pessoa's heteronymic schizophrenia—is it what you've dreamed of all your life? To paint a reclining something holding up on its goose-head hand the temper of horses ("too bad he can't draw figures") ("How strange it made me feel. One of the very great pictures of these last years")?

RETELL: "Turner could make very little of the human figure once it got too close."

We've heard your confession:

> Leaning over my inky cloak is no one of any color
> to give me in a short, plain, explanatory letter
>
> my *motivo* entire. Who pisses in the next urinal
> dares not look at me (the prick),
>
> possibly my past, *another swimmer of tepid waters.*

If the green bud you lacerate with your thumbnail while you talk to your idiot neighbor fails to remind you of poems of wattles made, still you could show more respect for nature, couldn't you, you who (RELATE) careless suck the drunken evening out of grapes, you, a barred Subject who takes charge, photographing "the sign of the undecidable" in the two nymphs asleep in nothing but one another's arms before, randy Faun, you tread on it?

> Listen, friend. I mean well by you:
> accept the perfect legibility of things,
>
> do not shake the blue boy till a little girl
>
> falls out, like a shattered fish
> of POORLY wrapped pencils,
>
> and the angel with the telescope
> is blinded by the flow-blow

of leaves from her lungs. Who knows
how to enter everything possess

nothing and pass by? The trees

sway like the Ink Spots
singing "Your Feet's Too Big,"

then the WINDS of terror

no one forgets the traces of
carry the leaves of the pencils away.

## ACTIVE RHYTHM (Indigo Letter)

This artist, if you can call him an artist, was squirting blue paint out of his anus
      onto a canvas on the floor. I'm glad my mother wasn't there to see it.
It's what Messiaen calls active rhythm, as when one character
      punches another in the face.

                (There was a long pause.)
      "I have your order," Pieter said.
      "Where would you like it?"

      Went very still.
      "Don't wear the glass earrings, leave them on the table."

Classical art is the last car of the train, the one that goes by silently.
      It's like the thousands of silver crosses, too, that flash on the lake
without touching it. As for you, you paint with appalling carelessness:
      the road in your painting, if you can call it a road,
looks like chopped rotten wood. That does it, I use the word
      *crapulent* against you.
Tear my heart out, why don't you.

I have reviewed eight canvases this size and concluded: "Rain is junk atmosphere.
      It makes one detest all one's acquaintance."
Sometimes, amidst this decadent modern art, I tremble all over myself,
      a blind hairless dog at the base of a mountain of fleas
decomposing in twelve angles of fall.

You look surprised, you who feel at home
      in your air-hanger studio, hearing each up-in-the-corner
speaker howling the same meathead theory of art:
      "Lose modulation. Paint between things, not things."

      Just be a dove. Paint Venus pupping on your laundry bag
             *careless love*                *19*

## THE RED LETTER (Contemporary Poetry)

Myth, what is myth?

  : breath-pant of the rose. the panther of it departing.

What is poetry?

  : stern evaporative seating before a hole in a painted winter.

❊

Think of the muse's back, cold despite the blanket of canvas. Shirtless in the oil.

❊

"Art has become transparent to itself down to the very core, which is the constitutive nature of illusion" (Adorno). It dreams of being the toothpaste tube squeezed empty and torn open, to where the murderous shining is. But it is sticky still, with meaning it is sticky still.

❊

  The red in the lower right is a watcher, with that kind of nastiness.
  All the problems: Where is Thomas Wilcocks? Is the bedstead
  screwed to the floor?
  Can the  ghost of a white  horse  be startled  by a white horse?

  So postwar, these children
  licking their spinwheels in the sea wind.

❊

The work that leaves everyone confounded is precisely a work for everyone
(Badiou).

✻

But one wants to say to contemporary poetry: "Think of the Idea of water, the Idea of wind. See a person in the Idea see how he fits exactly there in Ithaca, at the edge of the campus, standing where the gray rain vomits on the gray water. As it is. As it was. Keep him in sight. Be a little human."

✻

Oneself always already wandered, how love the already wandered? (How love anything else?)

> If I were to write a letter I would think of very clear water
> but I would address to you any figure that stood out,
> everything that is oar-shaped, sharpened to cut
> through the nothing, sawing and whacking at it, if necessary,
>
> the jutting building
>
> on the left, oxide of chrome green roof edge,
> the horse's nasturtium-colored behind, the shirtless
>       rider,
> my blue boy, your hand still feeling along the wet eaves for the
>       stream's root,
> your right leg upright on the head of the distant blonde
>
> atheist in the market place, that's a masterpiece she's flossing
> married to a dentist, I wanted you to stay home.

## THE BLUE LETTER (the Plurality of the Baroque)

There's life in violet if you tear it asunder. It happens to have a
waggish behind. I think I could love the last
headland with brown's blue tent flying off it,
but not a *meant*.

As to your objection to Levinas
's suf-
focating goodness, what you play on your musical comb
is refutation enough.
I love it when you buzz with the plurality of the baroque.

~

Not that I'm happy, like *some* people. "The chase, the apprehension, the
grieving!" "Verlaine arrived here the other day, clutching a rosary. Three hours
later he had renounced his god and reopened the 98 wounds of Our Saviour."
As for me, I spent my headlights looking for another. How many are around me
here in the dark? Please, some one, help me find a stamp in this swamp.

~

There could be more canvas here, where
the chin is crushed and the field of vision just stops,/as when

your guardian removes his hand from your privates
because the house has made a coming sound,

but nice people don't ask for more.

~

"Clad in so much knowledge, he was overcome by deliberation, vacillation, and diffidence." Self-portrait on a tall rock, with self-inscribed personal testaments, ammunition, and a Somali grammar. "You could do me an enormous service: I am missing some essentials necessary for the creation of maps. am completely paralyzed. would like plenty of time to board."

I appreciate all you've done,
little though it was, I appreciate each and every one of you.
My dear papa, I hope you've learned some manners by now.
Tell me, is every dead mother so teeny she sings
from a radio tooth in a sweetheart's jaw?

~

"'If you desert my ship,' he said in loud, clear tones, 'you shall never come aboard again.'"

~

Not that I'm one to look back. I see blue as forward,
just as orange is rogue. How can you not love a blue pigeon
tree? The feathers are half air,
though the shit builds up around the trunk,

it's deep, isn't it? and does not go away, unlike

sexual things. Firstly I shoveled it to the margin.
Secondly I shaped it like a Bundt cake.
Thirdly I stand on it and scratch the pigeons' bellies,

I love it enormously that they purr.

# POLYESTER PERVERSITIES

#1

    In heavenly harmony fully de-thinged they came, the hours, mention of why declined, and went on their way as prettily as possible, not looking, swiftly easily on their way, their teeth laughing at the foretaste, more easily killed lying down, imagine the sounds of people eating together in another room, barbarians.

#2

    If I had a pet, my life said, *it wouldn't be you, it would be an intended thing.*

#3

    Childhood makes me speak incredulous to remember.

    I had been dancing a long time before I was one the two the many I was who came at me exacting plenty.

#4

    I lived like Frederick Church's *Sunset Evening in the West* stored lengthwise in the Seattle Art Museum, rounding its shoulders and holding still so as not to spill the two boys fishing from the boat. I loved the tiny woman in the red pioneer skirt lifting a bucket at the well then we were coming a leg over the fence like a cloud on a glass building and I look her in the face, jesus, and I ask do you have the time?

# YOU OBJECTS TO WHICH I GIVE THE ALWAYS LATE CHOIRS OF MY LOVE

### 1.

Light doesn't know you as I do, salad of many flavors, as up at my place I eat greens with my fingers when the chair doesn't let me down like water. But light's good to you ("Thinke not that I am come to destroye thee"), except when it's full of itself, as I am when I follow you like a thumping petard that would love you to pieces, just love you to pieces, my little Fannie Brawnes. I wish I had a better disposition.

### 2.

Never mind the stars, they're too far off to hurt you now, though light isn't light that hasn't already tossed you with a Pleiades of silver forks and spoons. It was long ago that I myself introduced into you the gas of abstraction, for I was a hurting particular not particular enough. I have consulted the doctors of philosophy. The asses, they said I had a meddlesome disposition.

### 3.

When I wake up, you return like feathers in my not any particular hair. Then I have to learn you all over again. At happy hour, I admire your rump roasts lined up on the bar stools at the Art Hotel. I wish I had a better disposition.

### 4.

In my first proposition concerning shadows I spoke of "luminous reverberation." I had been to the seashore, I was unstringing myself, no doubt wantonly. I apologize to you dear, dry things. Well, sometimes you're too dry; I tire of you. My father must have been a bore, I must have noticed that out of the corner of my eye.

## 5.

As if I'd married not the rude but the real, the moon tonight stops outside my window over the Arno, we're *together* over it, shining down on the inconstant play of forms. Those aren't alligator clips on the river, they're yellow pulses born only in these cataract fleet flash echoing snare beat Evelyn Glennie come to me on your bare feet I have praise for thee sorts of moments. This must be a weak, sweet hour in my disposition, as if the gap between ideas and the brute and nearly inside of me had been filled with a great compassionate sort of person growing lettuce, cucumbers, and tomatoes in mid air, a garden in the desert of the light.

## 6.

I think of the phrase *kindly disposition*. How it nods and nods. I think of it kindly.

## 7.

I wish I had a better education. I wish I were an exchange student, still a little green at the top, in the country of mortal cautions.

"NOTE THE WREATH OF HAIR AT WHICH THE BACK OF HER HEAD,
WHICH THOUGH FASTENED BY A SPIRLA OF FELLETS, ESCAPES
AT LAST AND FLIES OFF LOOSE IN A SWEEPING CURVE"

Water in its ruins I would surely sponge what I could.
But leaving out the differences on Friday there is some sense in that.
General or particular, you choose, dear, I have to sit down a minute
in the wounded operating sound of this breathing.

You ask, "Can you look into the eyes of a cornered rat
and listen to its chitter as you pick up a stone
without yourself becoming something small and terrified?"
Today, anyway, let me rest like metal strings softening to the rags

of a clavichord's *bing  bung*, so reminiscent, don't you think,
of musical glasses, in their "plaintive, disembodied, melancholy" tones?
Yet even if breathing's a pile in sequence, like rain,
shouldn't one try to connect up extremes in a mention like sailing

when, suddenly, the mast leans down and gulps salt
water without considering a single person's feelings?
I have an ache of excellent bits of many things, like a letter
for all the family, also days when no boat approaches to signal

your particular beauty on a background so purely unbreathing.

## YOUR BLUE HURTS OUR GREEN LIKE A LADDER POINTING
## THE WRONG WAY OUT OF RAW

so that "the beautiful 'phenomena' of life" we must endure. And who really wants
    a last unfaithful gawk at earth, as through a window at mountains grown so small
they're scraps on light's table, or to listen
    to the hero in his musky petunia shirt say once more,
"If I have eyes, it's to see what stands off from me
    like a great odor where the wound
still festers in the master of bronze"?

I knew then how he misunderstood the mission of the senses:

> Amiable riders, like trellis-work, approaching through the blossoming
>     almonds.

Saw how he trivialized the obscurity of the real:

> If someone asks, "Whose room is this?" say
> *"Match-claws broken."* Say *"The kettle blows a snow cloud."*
> Say: *"Lift the cup. Sniff: Orange spice."*

Why, then, aspire to be tall? To breathe (so suddenly it hurts)
    like a herb boat floating in steaming water
*we breathe when you take our weight presently entirely certainly tea.*

Tell us, hero, what you saw in the tale's deeply lacking air.

> "I saw humanity
> Joan-eyed in all the directions of fire."

# LEONARDO'S BICYCLE

Like Ceres trying to free her daughter
Before Jove clipped her, a queen card, to the spokes
Of light and dark, where she still flaps, stiff and sore,
You're married to one condition.

You could leave the island whose shore
You circle distractedly, your feet
Bleeding from its cut-tin-can-lid sharpness,
If you swam out beyond your three-chord

Grammar, as Scarlatti flew like a prince
On a weave-it-as-you-ride-it carpet
"Into remotest tonal regions," a
"Specialist in investigative harmony."

Leonardo drew a bicicletta
Of wood and metal, sleeker than his deck-
Umbrella flying machine.  Why should he build it?
It was born ideal, elegant, as image,

Or, from a bicycle thrown on its back
Like a wrestler, one could palm an alarming
Thrum, a double voluble revolution—
Like Beethoven, whose forms were as durable

As Haydn's but whose heart clouded with the genius
Of taking drama to be normal.  As it was,
Alas, for Proserpine, who, given a whirl,
Uttered ice on the down slope, heliotrope

At the top.  Which freed Ceres to hear Ar-
Ethusa's tale of terrified pursuit:
How, after she hung her clothes on a yielding
Willow bough and dove into the stream, she

Felt the River god's breath sweep enraptured
Through her hair, and screamed.  Whereupon divine
Ortygia doused the whole scene in fog, leaving
The god to thrash about blind in white night,

While he groped for her salmon calves, her otter back.
But then she became a cataract; she lived
A dramatic life.  As you would if you turned
So deaf a child's shriek from the street could make

You smile over your meal, which, as usual,
You eat alone, dipping a heel of bread
Into your soup, before you hear again,
Vivace e con brio, the precision

Of a rondo no brute instrument is spinning,
Resonant as a waterfall on an island,
Where, in the din and crash of the sensible,
Nymphs take off their clothes and die.

# MOZART'S SISTER

### 1

The piano's mahogany exaggeration
Gives you a second language, educated like a hill
Below which the ladies' voices, no Nymphenchor,
Pock guten tag in their lawn games hyacinthine.

There's no ca ca on these keys, is there, child,
Such as Brüder Hans says you should smell of?
Elegance is a white key and its shadow,
Precisely parallel—and, propped against

The piano-rest, a score releasing sound
Like a seaside market town, there's so much
Air there, and you there, also, anonymous,
The most silk.  Still, ta dum, there will come

A destruction, when like a compact cloud a felt
Hammer lands on all that's hooped and puffed
Opposite the conduct face.  Enter twilight
In its dirty underwear of marked-down china.

### 2

Alas, when you were born the sky was like pink
Staining the bath.  But when you learned to play
"With miraculous precision," you shone
As the included excluded third, father's toy

Automaton, applauded by princes,
Along with the wünderkind, the mocking boy.
Your left arm crossed under his right, you helped ignite
Notes that showed the summer light a way

Of holding a position with vast reception,
In glittering glass sections, like the palest
Surface scarf of a river, which, left to itself
As dusk darkens, grays from grasshopper green

To arsenic, and sitting by it sets to welling
The reproach of a beginning had no swelling:
A glove already clamped on one's narrow
Shoulder.  For the king's thugs are out, beetle black

Like those in Caravaggio's *Taking of Christ*,
Thought for so long to be a Hornhurst.  (The heart:
Is it a Caravaggio?  Thought to be Hornhurst?)
And now the chill evening has come, as in

"Word has been received of the death of
Michelangelo da Caravaggio,
The famous painter, following an illness in Port 'Ecole';
He was thirty-nine, without possessions, and alone."

## I TELL YOU THESE THINGS BECAUSE YOU ARE CLEARLY IN PAIN

### 1

. . . distances part themselves,      ovaries butchered;

       the rinsings of aluminum pails paling in the tons of stretch;
              ;

  is endless, that death;

and up close,
         the piles and pleats of you
  lying in the undivision.


### 2

Loose is the cloudblow that flows about you

—such work for the keel in you,
  as you plash, pale unface,
    into the dark.
          Can we be all ours a whole?

  "bearers of the unspeakable"      "bearers of the dew"


### 3

hush, now, the atomy sparks are humming. Is it a lull,
the lull of you? Somebody's breath
          making a little loving?

Which is not as if Fear-life disappears at the mass-curves,
nor as if you could taste up there

    the milk-swarms of the wild oars' glitter-talk,

   nor as if the moon,

       her pitted face
  high above a waste dotted far out with little sails,
          most
           dead/
         slumped,
  should call to us:

    "Such happiness,
  seeing you all different there, all at sea."

# THE NAME OF THE BOW

*The name of the bow* [bios] *is life* [bíos] *its work is death.*
—*Heraclitus*

This motor-heart, this leaf-fluke cutting the waters

      *noses of porpoise mercy     vapor slugs*

Clouds hanging over the mountains like sweetsmelling horse-dick lilacs from the
   garden wall, remember?

      *stick-swords    sticky honeysuckle    fresh chicken shit in the dark shed*

He had a keen look out, a detachment of twenty mothers, and still they took his
   leg to make Murphey, would ye, dance on nothing, now?

      *gleaming Virgil of the blackbirds    be gracious    delight in teaching*

What vain forms of matter are these who invent the Dream they're in, throwing
   up in the waters' troughs?

      *white-knuckle-foam    tumor-kelp    tubes for all the patients you've yet to be*

Death in the way the chief god in the painting points toward the sky
   over the picnic cloth, death in his beard's black virga

      *charred migrant's trousers in the chaff    tongue done radishing    roach-quick startles*

And still he raced across the heath of signs to ask why assassinated

      *darkening white horse    run at me    sweating the day's odors*

## BEGUN BEGUN IS ANYTHING MORE VIOLENT SPONTANEOUS FAITHFUL?

Who's that man walking ahead of us, striking butterflies together like stones?
    Is it the one they call—the master of tears? Never mind, the California
quail, plucking the sage brush, wears his astonishment—on his head,

and I agree—now that I'm back where everything is water
    with a drop of writing in it, floating. Ancient rhythms, nod
to your American brothers, who wipe rib sauce on their aprons

with fingers of cook-out—fingers of good grief. First, blood
    understands—my hero with a shoe of pirate, and a shoe of harbor.
Then words—tear at the trees'—hair in the wood pulp of the page,

helicopter shuddering down to take out the living and the dead.
    The dead! . . . Clarified like Botticelli's veils the tears of things—
spume away. Big boy like water sport? Little splash up?—

                    mariner, already the fountain is wilder.

The woman who lost her goat—fed its image every day;
    but, really, it was nothing like. Get into the car—kiss
the denim where it splits—over my knee. I could seize you like a stiff—

honey comb—could crush you—drip your goodness over me,
    but could I ever find—the exact—same—sweetness again,
distinct as a fly on the tongue? Everything dies like a streakworm

three leagues from the early moon. The Ella lights adieu—the Sid,
    the Jack lights adieu—adieu the Sloan. What will be asked of you,
the darkness said, is to beat—back madness, you who eat

everything you can find—brick or redder—because the air
  has no patient perfume. And should that tall man turn around
on the trail, as the Big Bear hunts the blueberry's

sea-green meat before he sleeps—will you say:
  I am ready to go? After the Thelma lights, the Iva Dell,
the Molly, the Vanessa, the Joan?

## BANANA PEAKS GET SNOWFALL (the Equinox is Coming Closer
like Ice Cream)


Alice does not Carroll to take the banana boat to Paris, there is such
Eiffel distrust of resemblance there. (When the monkey rains
dig their furred forks into the snow, Parisians say, the Seine
goes bananas, like a lot of women schtupped in the white
Calcuttas of translation.)  What is wrong, give me the keys,
give me the bananas, I could make a hand of them, I could
hurriedly to the podium the topic is unexpected, my eight
scoops of white gauze from the Medical Corps.

Will no one lean out from a window in the All-
at-once, like an interested banana? Why do I even ask your black
spots to meet me in the clinic of the unmarketable dark?
The last of the sacred, "the submission of flesh to flesh":
sweetness extreme, banana cream: twice
in the yellow balcony seats (scrooch down, honey)
during the classification and treatment of war wounds.

Alfred North Whitehead cannot bear Alfred South Whitehead
—it is too much reality. To be more, and less, than one.
Turn me around, somebody. Process me, West to East,
I do not like the way I go in my good year
rubber shoes. Find a song for the last mile: our buffalo heads
long to be herds of bananas sniffing dawn's blood.
Alice not warm here in the crook of my arm
while my other arm smells of distant (and coming closer) ice cream.

# "RAGS-AND-BLOOD-SUNSET"

The pooch in Velazquez's *Las Meninas*
is impatient with posing. Besides, a girl

is stepping on him: she's the smallest child
in the painting and wants to be noticed.

As who does not? Most do not
because it makes them feel guilty. To be caught

existing, it's presumptuous
and marks you out for death. It's better to stay

on the scaffold side of the canvas, which
in *Las Meninas* is too close to the front

of the scene, exposed, unless one stands
far to the left. There. Are we safe now?

What shall we do? Sex might be good,
it's so private. Well, nothing's more public

in a sense, if someone else is looking
at your long underwear with you in it

and wondering  could it contain the final
vertigo, which is never final, anyway.

Besides, nails, hip bones, teeth, print themselves
on the quiffy skin, like the tracks of Rommel's

Mk IV's or Eisenhower's jeep driven
by his mistress, Skibereen or the dints

men make as they lie on their backs and kick
at jammed rifle bolts on Algerian sand.

But the girl knows nothing of this. One day,
alone in her room, she'll study her leg

in the mirror. Is the mirror bored? She feels
it likes to look at her. Foolish girl, to

give herself to death like that, moaning.

# SHOW ME A GOOD TIME, WILD THING, YOU KNOW YOU HAVE THAT REPUTATION

I had me an upper joy once.
      My blister-skinned boy had "PV,"
"V" for "vulgaris." No one else would touch him
      (after the women in town undressed him,
they'd scream), he was that beautiful to me.
What Venus rose from the sea to see I saw in him plain,
unlatched like a mockingbird's metal singings.

My suppurating boy must have affection was afflicted to go on.
The mystery of a person who puts on his glasses
and reads a book by the table lamp, reads and
                    reads!
Interrupted asked would I let him breathe said
I can't I'm the crimson fringe of you, this fire.

Can a man bear the sound of an empty trailer before opening the door from
outside
where the Jeffrey pines raise their arms
to the terrible minor of the air?

Voluptua? I've been there.
    Hear them? The pipes hot goat pipes a great stove of birds shrilling.

The nine brightnesses the Greeks tell of—if I could find them
  I'd say,
        *put down your lamps, beautiful bitches, and offer your stomachs to the starry*
*terror—*
        *will show you a good time— is why you are here.*

Death starts from the sergeant's stripes in the wrists, the chevrons of blue veins.

So you take the night shamelessly against the wall,
the cold whip of the wind, the whiffled hair —

                        slips down and crawls away,

                                 *and all will be taken —*

I'm going to find some lippy kid will tie my wrists behind me and drive me
into the mountains
                 —a gypsy boy
to stamp out the last of my face's fire.

When I think of that I get hard as a rotten pumpkin's scabrous stem —
        good for chucking the whole mess.

        *(. . . A white tennis shoe by the side of the road.*

                        *A little while, child,*
*and all will be taken —)*

## SCENES FROM THE NOVEL *GARDEN OF THE GREEN NIGHTINGALES*

~ X finds documents in the trunk of Marta's car. She is the Red Hand. (*white solitudes of retreating ankles; her chilly composure*)

~ "real": yes she has real attractions: synonyms; antonyms. (*yellow flickers in her eyes     fire in the hobo camp by the railroad tracks*)

~ p. 29: X imagines her velvet mandoline, as is his wont when wine is a swallow and his cup shakes out its shepherd curls.

~ In the Red Hand's notes, allusions to @. But, X says, we violate her who turn up her palms, sniffing.

~ "I can't bear to have you looking at my handwriting," Marta objects, "the rearing knuckles, the small crab-jointed bones, the so-squamous genes."

~ p. 181: A whistle from a high rock in Fiesole. The Red Hand, probably, at the narrow end of the nightingale's tongue.

~ X lives down there, in the black drop, his teeth gleaming when he wants to be charming.

~ p. 201: "I would laugh if I were a woman," he said, "mother moons spanking the naked bottoms of the tree tops, *ecriture* deliriums"

~ "When I wrote my novel under the red tile roof under the red planet under the crescent moon in Firenze, in the Clinic of the Third Witch with the Rabbit," Marta confides, "I signed myself Sideways Leaner Hooting Down a Rolled-Paper Tube. I loved you like nobody then."

~ p. 253: X feels like a noun decomposing in the intestines of the chapter, though the words around him chatter in the wings of a beauty pageant, one just remembering to spit out her gum, which had gone flat anyhow. "The smell of death is my Gethsemane," he thinks. Slowly he repeats the sentence. "I am ready to begin my novel."

~ X fears he was altered in a moment of distraction, like the spider *P. argyra*, which, injected with psychosis by a wasp, spins a limp clothesline, under market value, on which the wasp children hang until they're old enough to eat her. (The spider "sits still in the middle" of its web, "waiting to be killed.")

   "You are all of that to me," Marta says. "No to nations. I like liberty."

~ p. 388: Night after night, X screens *Notorious*. Is he Claude Raines or Cary Grant? How long can he stay here, in the insensitivity of black and white?

~ p. 400: ("Pale he was as he crossed the bridge," she wrote, "like an alarm clock set to wake in another story.")

~ p. 421: X touches a red ant in the gleam-light of the china vase. Yes, only painted. He dreams of lime light dropping like shade in the garden of the green nightingales.

~ p. 422: X plants documents in the trunk of Marta's car.

~ When he pushes her Fiat into the Arno, it "breaks up into red tears."

~ "A dark veil is not a net," says the note left on his pillow.

~ X sits out the night in the Cafe Nightingale in the smoky croak of its splintered pipe.

# PROPAGATION IN AN ARITHMETIC OF WINGS

Who was to carry me over
        oh with the crust removed?

Who was to field of?

One singing. Strawberry vowels.

I knew one who stayed "1" like an unplugged clock.
From there she looked around.

Her dog stared from the gray carpet.

I called her Virginia. Virginia ice on the road.
V as in the bow of a ship backing off,

twin anchors aloft in the eyeholes.

Two do not go into one and live.
I wish I were a balcony on how many sides.
Let me kiss three, no, seven, oh,
how many civilians were killed?

I only wanted to bright hot bell puff undone
in my gangbuster curls,

just a little. With her. Just a squeeze.

She never touched her dog,
a black thing, panting.

# "HEARTS IN WHICH THE MOVEMENTS OF WORLDS ARE BOUND AND RUPTURED"

The eyes of cickens, pretty lunations, and you, do you light up the fruit?
Though you meant to scale the hairy cliffs of raspberry-colored syllables,
who are you but masked voice speaks sliddery
on perverse side of screen?

                    Nor are they with you, the sacred touchers,
like the white inner tissues sailing south in the milkweed,
though weed you are, not ripe hip of Florida
                     in the peregrine-hearted yellow squash seed.

In wooden boxes the color of the sun's
urine (orange-dark, sickroom stink , don't turn away, not this time),
they are beating on the walls—how many? so many?—
the likes you would not stop yesterday to carry.

Across and across cerise your breath draws the black streak
of the last conversation you had before you woke to find her
dead: "I don't know. Two o'clock? Three? Try to sleep."

Hearts in which the movements of worlds are bound and ruptured
all unbound now and whose this whim whose dead groves
what birds startle when the copper leaves rush at them?

      Shadow mounts the top row of windows in the Palazzo Vecchio;
                    mounts the oversized clock; mounts the tower.
And you,
        heart like a long scissor,
were you here with her
                 that first summer after college?
Can you not remember were you nobody sensible?

*The pizzeria's coral table cloths, the red*
*geraniums, the table lamps slightly*
*brighter in the withering daylight, like loudening frogs —*

do they look familiar? And if they did?

How late it is to fetch back the pearls, those unpracticed swimmers,
scattered now in the movements of the worlds.

# THE RED AWFUL DARKNESS INSIDE THE WORLD

The news shocks you like lightning stutter-
  stepping in the slower staccato of your
breathing. First you're white in it,
  then black. I can't find you in all that char.

Why can't you be . . . I say you *are* a lake
  so Montana the cohoes arch like saddles
when they pump out heathenish destructions
  of endings. I say it. I put it upon you

unfairly. To be like that, down to water's
  very belly, the mixed colors of milk
and geraniums. Muscling the good cycles;
  silent mouth open in a voice all resembling.

You tell me of a woman taxi driver killed in
  Baghdad today. Maybe she hadn't heard the guards?
Maybe she was singing or thinking of her daughters?
  I don't now how burnt flesh smells, you say, but the

smell of burnt hair is dark brown and liver and foul
  and unforgivable and California smells of sea
and lemon and New England of cold apples in a cellar.
  *I can't bear this country, its self-satisfied virtues.*

You say that worse will come, people everywhere
  biting each other, faces hideous with rage.
You say the inside of the country's as pink as a pork chop.
  Pink as a cheek struck by a strap. Pink as a bosom

before it becomes all red and juicy.

Before it is red in a most offensive manner.
Red behaving strangely. Red as five bay horses
    rearing screaming foaming and shivering

in a drawer in the Oval office. Red
    as the husband and wife killed by a convoy
outside Baghdad. Red as the candy that
    burst from their candy truck and lay in the road.

Red as the tongues of the soldiers who hadn't eaten
    in 24 hours. Who eyed the spill.
Who ate the candy.

# THE WHITE LETTER

We are a fair people, white headlights of people, who have loved the north,
the east, the south, the west out of all reason, a curious people,

        picking out the others in the barbarous
        see-through of the falls, and I regret to say
        the pond in the orchard is now full of them.

        I have so loved your views of the working people,
        gold earrings in the little brown girls' ears.
        Write to me when the Flake White

        peeling from your thighs
        has been diagnosed.

Re: the cloudhooves of the love that safeguards the universe, crossing the
Rockies, what are you thinking, don't tell me, *the women & Childn. Cried dureing
my Stay of an hour at this place* and a still whiter thought is always yet to come *to
interigate thro' the Intptr.*, just as America leapt out of "cloudy, moist, melancholy
old Europe," spilling six feet of nice young men into Kentuck—

        and certainly land washed by packing-peanut surf
        conveys a rich position. Always
        the power of white is exciting to me.
        the creaming edge of the Pacific
        is the childhood of someone white,
        laughing to herself now,
        she's that kind of titanium—
        riding into combers on a mount
        the pale color of pilgrim time.
        Still, we'll want props if we're to fuck again:
        lickable polished policewoman shoes

and a white sheet like a mountain stream
to tighten around the throat.

*I undertook to tell the Cheif who we wer, how come, wither, and rolled up my sleve to shew him I was not a Savage and did not wish to hirt him. He threw his left arm over my wright sholder and vociforated the word* âh-hí-a, âh-hí-a, *"I am much rejoiced." He requested his Squar might be used for the night.*

*I had this day an agility. A beautiful howling green down to the river below. Named the river Dearborn after the Secretary of war,*

and unto us this evening,
several hundred miles within difficult going,
this wild & mountainous bosom of more.

# LOS BARBARIANS DEL NORTE

(after Samuel Chamberlain's *My Confession: Recollections of a Rogue*, a memoir of the Mexican War)

My rangers rode to washboard banjos when all nature seemed a graceful group of señoritas sobbing in the shade of orange trees. I could have been a conscience in those days, but I lassoed the wooden Savior and dragged him through the plazula, like the villagers dun me and skinned me besides.

On the night of my burial "it is a hot summer evening" there was 60 of me in the pine box talking small seethe like fingernails strumming absentmindedly on a washboard. I jumped out and with a spunky "Hebe" wore no stockings painted the wild figures of "la Jarabe," while the flamenco flounce of starlight caught at the feet of the drummer boy.

Maj. Bliss asked would I make a clean breast of everything. "Major," I said, "light my ducteen with your har" (Reader, *sabe que es pulque*?) and executed a flank movement on the dining room table and gained a good if bloody position. No mustard in Mexico could overtake my Kentuck past two rivers kept my course by the stars. But seven of me were found under a tenderloin steak with Ramonda our earless prize and damnably dealt with.

Our dragoons played poker with money from the corpses whose marble eyes was watching them in the moonlight. Next day in Saltillo an Escopette ball passed through the cantles of my saddle and emasculated me. I asked the government for $10,000 recompense who had given my all in a country of chaparral justice when life was a crayon stump for to paint a naked Senorita on a washboard.

Fifty of me was sentenced to be hanged at the village of San Angel, four was hanged at Mixcoac, and six more sang at the Fortress of Chapultepec, standing on a wagon like a storm, its arms and legs black from being tied off. But I said "I will live to eat the goose that will fatten on the grass that grows on yer own grave, Colonel, and on the graves of Quitman, Twiggs, and Worth," and we swung out then and danced we danced like flushed and florid Florida men.

Oh we was ripe and exhuberant as any could wish to look upon *the breaths of the frightened flew before us* on the trail was life then, our hats occupied and arisen.

# THE LAST PACKARD UNTIL WE WIN THE WAR

*Life*, April 16, 1945. Ike's massive forehead. Creases I hiked in my Poll-Parrot shoes. Rosebud mouth is especially bad on round faces. Full mouth becomes Barbara Nelson. Seventeen shells have hit in target area (above).

>*Child, you could be such a piece of celerity and joy, a pinwheel whirring over this republic of coming and going grasshopper lights crossing in a glaring gangland thatch of straw-golden scratch-field.*

>*But you sleep like a warm smell on a metal world.*

This is how he looked when U. S. troops freed him last week. Exaggerated mouth looks bad on lean faces. This one's right for Carolyn Kasler. The men open their mouths to lessen the concussion on their ear drums. The laughs of a nation. Of all American traits none is more characteristic than our universal appreciation of comedy.
"I want bags," General Bradley said. "Bags, bags, bags."

>*"Whoever desires something infinite does not know what he desires."*

>*O clouds   did you see?   my vulture of syringes   captured at the Border.*

On D Day, a jeep must be ready to roll the instant the ship grounds, and thanks to Veedol motor oil, it is. The happier you are, the lovelier you are. "Fresh up"—keep smiling!  You've been in a gray fog since the day he went away—half-seeing, half-hearing, hardly daring to hope. Then the sun floods in . . . your man is yours . . . you're *his*. Here at Community we'll have the finest silverplate for you in a world beyond the shadow of war . . . patterns that brides have ever loved.

>*Homeless drifts in the cloudways of destruction,*
>>*you do not know who you are.*

The house we'll build when you come home. Blown dams farther south. And a kitchen for me full of magical things. One slice of bread unpeeled potatoes one bowl of pea soup per day. Buy war bonds, BEST RETURN ON YOUR DOLLAR. Man who has just come up trail is bending over to keep out of sight. Promise yourself you'll keep your hands as thrillingly lovely as they are now.

*"larks over the death cells
militarism progressing westward"*

On the Burma road, a fresh, flavorful Camel cigarette is just like a taste of home. Keep a jeep in shape for the Japs. Rosebud mouth is especially bad on round faces. A ringing challenge. An awesome responsibility. You decreed, years ago, that these lives be saved when you first demanded "U.S." Rubber Products. A "rocket serenade" against Japanese on Okinawa.

*Only the holy remains intact without a location, do you see?
Like language opened up at great depth. Can you imagine?*

"Good heavens, man," Miss Stein said, "don't worry so much! You must smile at somebody—it's shameful. Twent-five years ago you all had broad grins on your faces all day long. The French are very disappointed. Last time everybody was drunk all the time. All right, you'll have to go to the Pacific. In the Pacific you'll have people to smile at too—not Japs [waving her finger]—nobody wants to smile at Japs—but there are Chinamen—Chinamen are kindly people too. What I am getting at is that in this horrible war we're in danger of losing our humanity."

*Where there are no gods, phantoms
wander in the cloudways.
Hatred's dispersals. Do you see now?*

The new skills of war. The building of a greater, happier nation, where all men and women will have the chance to make their dreams come true.

I know it will be just the way your letters describe it to me.

# COME IN, KANSAS CITY, COME IN, PLEASE

While herself is ruby slippered in pomegranate seeds in the dark beneath
      the plains, killing time,
who is gardening in the heartland? A poet I knew outside Allegory
woke to find the icy night still sore at the horizon mouth,
then lay back on a pillow purple from the brown-hearted grapes of his hair.

Americans, do you want me to go on?

Yes, tell us more about the heartland.

In summer the people herd large roses into the beens of childhood.
And the corn trembles on its thin ankles, like Chihuahuas.

What else?

After rains, the sun holds up the smoking scalp of the prairie.
And the old ones remember wide rivers so fine no one crossed them,
unrolling like sheets of Reynolds Wrap before it's slathered with apple crumb
      betty pie.
The good folk camped on the banks like trees
and watched the shining republic of desire roll by.

Tell us more.

Today, a deputy caught two boys drag racing on riding mowers down Main St.
in Ellston, Iowa, whereas in Tegucigalpa
the dog-boys sniff shoe glue to survive the cold nights
and no one stops them, in their seed time.

# THE YELLOW LETTER

He was battered out from his stay in the infantry.
Ran his knife through the ear of a walkie-talkie, called it
"Getting the President's Attention." We fear he will never return

to the dishevelment of ambiguity. It's like watching Ted Koppel's
mother combing his hair on Nightline. All the Iraqi
POWs wanted to talk about, someone said, was bananas.

We may never again be cracked up to be.
I'm so afraid to losing you, who don't give a shit no more.
I miss something to go crazy about. I wish I had

a bowl of sparrows to feed to. I wish I could speed
somebody's beauty around. The tush of George W.
Bush is singing from our cabana: he called this one

"Singing Full-Throated from the Oval Room."
And now for my imitation of waving wands of corn
in the land you loved so well, back in the eventide

letting darkness down easy.

# PROPAGATION OF THE USA

"This Chamber is silent—ominously, dreadfully silent. There is no debate, no discussion, no attempt to lay out for the nation the pros and cons of this particular war. This nation is about to embark upon the first test of a revolutionary doctrine: the doctrine of preemption. The idea that the United States or any other nation can legitimately attack a nation that is not imminently threatening but may be threatening in the future is a radical new twist on the traditional idea of self-defense. . . . Yet this chamber is hauntingly silent."

# PROPOGATIOON IN A SCRAMBLER RADIO

> *Il fit beugler Achille . . . , Il fit hurler la reine Clytemnestre.*
> —Marmontel

It is a bugle, Achilles. It hurls the Clytemnestra rain.

# NOTES

**What Though Your Daddy's Trumpet Is Buttered Toast** ends with a quotation from the photographer David Wojnarowicz's book *Brush Fires in the Social Landscape*.

**Alison Thank You For Your Question** adapts Walter Benjamin's *Arcades Project* and echoes Frank O'Hara's comment, in his *Art Chronicles*, on a well-trained soprano's scream.

**"You Can Be the Subject of Wild Admiration in Ten Days"** takes its title from Gertrude Stein.

**The Green Letter** quotes Patrick Heron on the painter Turner.

**You Objects to Which I Give the Always Late Choirs of My Love** revises the valence of a phrase from James Clarence Mangan's translation of Schiller's *Die Ideals*: "All my Divinities have died of grief, / And left me wedded to the Rude and Real."

**"Note the Wreath of Hair . . ."** borrows its title from John Ruskin's *Mornings in Florence*.

**Banana Peaks Get Snowfall** ends with an image from a letter to the author by 'Annah Sobelman.

**Active Rhythm** is indebted to Gilles Deleuze's comment (in his book *Francis Bacon*) that abstract painting was anticipated "every time a great painter of the past stopped painting things in order 'to paint between things,'" which is in turn indebted to Élie Faure's discussion of Velasquez in his *History of Art*, vol. 4, *Modern Art*.

**Leonardo's Bicycle** quotes Donald Tovey on Scarlatti and echoes a couple of phrases from Ovid's *Metamorphoses*, book v. A model of Leonardo's bicycle was included in an exhibition of constructions based on some of his designs in Fiesole (and elsewhere) in 2002.

**Mozart's Sister** ends with a quotation from Sergio Benedetti's *Caravaggio: The Master Revealed* (published by the National Gallery of Ireland).

**"Hearts in Which the Movements of Worlds are Bound and Ruptured"** borrows its title from Georges Bataille's book *The Inner Experience*.

**"Rags-and-Blood Sunset"** takes its title from a short story by Annie Proulx.

**The Last Packard Until We Win the War** quotes, of course, from the April 16, 1945 issue of *Life* magazine; also from Ezra Pound's *Pisan Canto (LXXIV)*.

**Propagation of the USA** is a quotation (with elisions) from Senator Robert Byrd's senate floor speech, Feb. 12, 2002.

**Propagation in a Scrambler Radio** performs a sight-misreading of lines of Marmontel's (in English: "He makes Achilles . . . roar, he makes Clytemnestra scream").

Also Available from saturnalia books:

LETTERS TO POETS: CONVERSATIONS ABOUT POETICS, POLITICS, AND COMMUNITY
edited by Jennifer Firestone and Dana Teen Lomax

FAMOUS LAST WORDS by Catherine Pierce
WINNER OF THE SATURNALIA BOOKS POETRY PRIZE 2007

DUMMY FIRE by Sarah Vap
WINNER OF THE SATURNALIA BOOKS POETRY PRIZE 2006

CORRESPONDENCE by Kathleen Graber
WINNER OF THE SATURNALIA BOOKS POETRY PRIZE 2005

THE BABIES by Sabrina Orah Mark
WINNER OF THE SATURNALIA BOOKS POETRY PRIZE 2004

MIDNIGHTS
Poems by Jane Miller / Artwork by Beverly Pepper
ARTIST/POET COLLABORATION SERIES NUMBER FOUR

STIGMATA ERRATA ETCETERA
Poems by Bill Knott / Artwork by Star Black
ARTIST/POET COLLABORATION SERIES NUMBER THREE

ING GRISH
Poems by John Yau / Artwork by Thomas Nozkowski
ARTIST/POET COLLABORATION SERIES NUMBER TWO

BLACKBOARDS
Poems by Tomaz Salamun / Artwork by Metka Krasovec
ARTIST/POET COLLABORATION SERIES NUMBER ONE

*DAYS OF UNWILLING* was printed using the fonts Cochin and Berthold
Akzidenz-Grotesk.

www.saturnaliabooks.com